DPT

WORLD ALMANAC® LIBRARY OF THE MIDDLE AGES

the plague and medicine

IN THE MIDDLE AGES

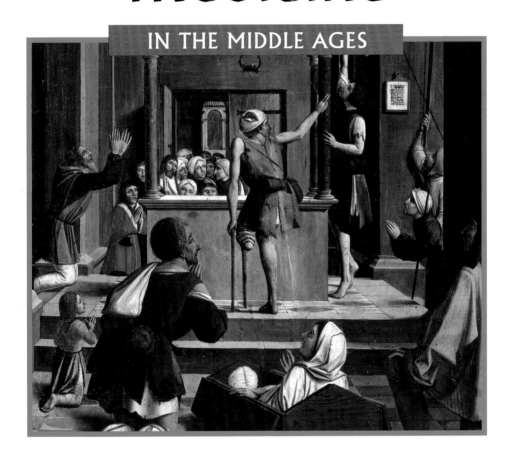

FIONA MACDONALD

WORLD ALMANAC® LIBRARY

Please visit our web site at: www.worldalmanaclibrary.com
For a free color catalog describing World Almanac® Library's list of high-quality books
and multimedia programs, call 1-800-848-2928 (USA) or 1-800-387-3178 (Canada).
World Almanac® Library's fax: (414) 332-3567.

Library of Congress Cataloging-in-Publication Data

Macdonald, Fiona.
    The plague and medicine in the Middle Ages / by Fiona Macdonald.
      p. cm. — (World Almanac Library of the Middle Ages)
    Includes bibliographical references and index.
    ISBN 0-8368-5898-0 (lib. bdg.)
    ISBN 0-8368-5907-3 (softcover)
    1. Plague—History—Juvenile literature. 2. Medicine, Medieval—
History—Juvenile literature. I. Title. II. Series.
    RC172.M337 2005
    614.5'732'0094—dc22   2005040783

First published in 2006 by
World Almanac® Library
A Member of the WRC Media Family of Companies
330 West Olive Street, Suite 100
Milwaukee, WI 53212 USA

Copyright © 2006 by World Almanac® Library.

Produced by White-Thomson Publishing Ltd.
Editor: Walter Kossmann
Volume editor: Peg Goldstein
Designer: Malcolm Walker
Photo researcher: Amy Sparks
World Almanac® Library editorial direction: Valerie J. Weber
World Almanac® Library editor: Jenette Donovan Guntly
World Almanac® Library art direction: Tammy West
World Almanac® Library graphic design: Kami Koenig
World Almanac® Library production: Jessica Morris and Robert Kraus

Photo credits:
Akg-Images: pp. 4 (Musée du Petit Palais, Paris), 5, 38, 42 (Akg), 7 (Erich Lessing), 8, 12, cover and
pp. 13, 24, 34, 41 (British Library), 9 (Musée Condé, Chantilly), 14 (Biblioteca Estense, Modena), 15
(Bibliothèque Royale, Brussels), 16 (Musée Condé, Chantilly), 19 (Bibliothèque Nationale, Paris), 20,
22, 32 (Austrian National Library), title page and pp. 25 (Galleria Nazionale, Rome/Nimatallah), 29
(Bibliothèque Nationale, Paris/Jerome da Cunha), 35 (Alte Pinakothek, Munich); Art Archive: pp. 26
(Biblioteca Augusta, Perugia/Dagli Orti); Bridgeman Art Library: pp. 11 (Archives Charmet), 21
(British Library), 23 (Galleria dell' Accademia, Venice), 27 (Ospedale di Santa Maria della Scala,
Siena/Alinari), 31 (Bibliothèque Municipale, Reims), 33 (University of Bologna Collection), 37
(National University Library, Prague/Giraudon), 40 (Musée Atger, Faculté de Médecine, Montpellier/
Giraudon), 43 (British Museum); Topfoto: p. 17.

*Cover: A bishop blesses monks covered with boils from the plague in this illumination from c. 1360.
Title page: In this fifteenth-century painting, pilgrims pray for cures at Saint Sebastian's tomb.*

Printed in Canada

1 2 3 4 5 6 7 8 9 09 08 07 06 05

Contents

Words that appear in the glossary are printed in **boldface** type the first time they occur in the text.

Source References on page 45 give bibliographic information on quoted material. See numbers (¹) at the bottom of quotations for their source numbers.

he Middle Ages are the period between ancient and early modern times—the years from about A.D. 500 to 1500. In that time, Europe changed dramatically. The Middle Ages began with the collapse of the **Roman Empire** and with "**barbarians**" invading from the north and east. In the early years of the Middle Ages, western European farmers struggled to survive. This period ended with European merchants eagerly seeking new international markets, European travelers looking for fresh lands and continents unknown to them to explore, European artists creating revolutionary new styles, and European thinkers putting forward powerful new ideas in religion, government, and philosophy.

What Were the "Middle Ages" Like?

Some people view the period as the "Dark Ages," an era marked by ignorance and brutality. It is true that **medieval** people faced difficult lives marred by hard work, deadly diseases, and dreadful wars, but their lives included more than that.

The Middle Ages were also a time of growing population, developing technology, increasing trade, and fresh ideas. New villages and towns were built; new fields were cleared; and, with the help of new tools like the wheeled iron plow, farms produced more food. **Caravans** brought silks and spices from faraway lands in Asia. New sports and games, such as soccer, golf, chess, and

playing cards, became popular. Musicians, singers, acrobats, and dancers entertained crowds at fairs and festivals. Traveling troupes

◀ Doctors examine injured soldiers in a hospital tent close to a battlefield. From left to right, they are counting a pulse, looking at a urine sample, and cleaning a flesh wound. This picture was painted in France in the early fifteenth century.

performed plays that mixed humor with moral messages for anyone who would stop and listen.

Religion, education, and government all changed. Christianity spread throughout Europe and became more powerful. Another major faith—Islam—was born and carried into Europe from the Middle East. New schools and universities trained young men as scholars or for careers in the Church, medicine, and the law. Medieval rulers, judges, and ordinary citizens created **parliaments**, jury trials, and the common law. These changes in the fabric of society still shape our world today.

Historians divide the entire period into two parts. In the early Middle Ages, from about A.D. 500 to 1000, Europe adjusted to the changes caused by the fall of the Roman Empire and the formation of new kingdoms by Germanic peoples. In these years, the Christian Church took form and Europeans withstood new invasions. In the late Middle Ages, from about 1000 to 1500, medieval life and culture matured. This period saw population growth and economic expansion, the rise of towns and universities, the building of great cathedrals and mosques, and the launching of the **Crusades**.

An Uncertain Life

Medieval writers often described a character called "Lady Fortune." They pictured her spinning a large wheel to which all human lives were tied. At one moment, a person might be rich, proud, powerful, well fed, safe, healthy, and happy. With another spin of her wheel, Lady Fortune could turn the same person's life upside down. Then they would suddenly become poor, weak, hungry, afraid, ill, and alone.

Lady Fortune did not exist, of course. She was just a symbol of medieval people's fears. They could understand how some misfortunes happened: farm crops might fail, or countries might be devastated by war. Many other troubles remained mysterious, though. In particular, medieval people did not know what caused illness or how to cure it.

▲ Lady Fortune is pictured in an Italian manuscript painted around 1450. She is blindfolded to show that she treats all people equally and is seated at the center of her turning wheel. To the left, a man clings tightly to the wheel, hoping to rise in the world and gain riches and power. To the right, a man falls down, away from Fortune's favor.

This book describes some of the most serious illnesses affecting medieval people, including a terrible outbreak of **plague**—one of the worst natural disasters the world has ever seen. It also explores the ways in which doctors, traditional healers, and religious leaders all tried to bring comfort to sick people and cure disease.

CHAPTER 1

Living and Dying

ompared with today's population, medieval Europe was relatively empty. Only about eighty million people lived there in the 1340s before the Black Death struck, a mere 10 percent of today's population. Even so, it is doubtful whether the land could have supported many more people because it was not possible to grow more food with medieval farming technology.

A Growing Population

About 75 percent of European families worked on farms; about 10 percent were merchants or skilled craftspeople; about 10 percent were professionals and gentry; and about 5 percent were nobles. Professionals, **gentry**, and nobles formed the governing classes.

Throughout the early Middle Ages, the population increased. Forests were cut down; marshes were drained, and moorland was cleared to create fields to grow food to feed more families. Trade, travel, and manufacturing developed and supported many thousands of people who lived and worked in seaports, cities, and towns.

By about 1300, however, there was little spare land. Some parts of Europe, such as southeastern England and the Low Countries (now Belgium and the southern Netherlands), were badly and uncomfortably overcrowded.

Food prices increased because there were so many mouths to feed. At the same time, wages fell because there were not enough jobs to go around. Trapped between high prices and low wages, people became poorer and poorer. After about 1300, many Europeans lived on the edge of starvation. In good years, peasant farmers produced enough to feed their families plus a small surplus to sell. Laborers also took home a living wage. In bad years, however, farmers had to eat their **seed corn** and breeding animals. People without land or jobs lost their homes and became beggars. They **scavenged** for wild foods, hoped for charity, and prayed.

Besides enduring hunger, poor people were at extra risk from bad weather—especially freezing winters—and from disease. **Leprosy**, **malaria**, **dysentery**, **tuberculosis**, and other potentially fatal illnesses were widespread in Europe in

Medieval People—on Average

	Men	Women
Height	5 feet 7 inches (1.7 meters)	5 feet 2 inches (1.57 m)
Married	yes	yes
Age at marriage	about 18	between 14 and 20
Number of children	between 3 and 5	between 3 and 5
Likely occupation	Peasant farmer	Housewife/laborer
House	2 rooms, earthen floor, open fire, yard	
Land	10–30 acres (4–12 hectares) for the whole family	
Health	Bone disease, worms, injuries, fleas	
Appearance	Disabilities, scars likely	

▲ This tender portrait of an old man and a young boy from a wealthy family was painted by Italian artist Domenico Ghirlandaio in 1488. The old man's nose is misshapen by a skin disease that medieval medicine could not cure.

medieval times. There were outbreaks of a mysterious illness called "sweating sickness" and influenza. Many people suffered from scabies (an itchy, disfiguring skin infection spread by tiny mites) and intestinal worms. Even simple colds—and the chest infections that often followed them—could be killers.

Diet and Health

Food could also cause bad health. Rich people's meals were lavish but unbalanced. They ate too much meat (which gave them digestive upsets), honey (which rotted their teeth), and not enough fruits or vegetables. They also drank strong wine. Poor people ate large amounts of bread with cheese or peas, beans, and other vegetables. This diet was healthier than the diet of the rich—if they could get enough food. They drank weak ale, which was safer than untreated water because it was boiled during brewing.

▲ Here English men drink wine and sing in about 1430. At the front of the picture, a young servant is filling a jug with more wine from a huge wooden barrel. A small dog and pet monkeys (symbols of foolishness and bad behavior) play nearby.

Living Conditions

Medieval people liked to be clean and hoped to be healthy. They took it as a compliment to be called "fresh" or "sweet." Nevertheless, in spite of their best efforts, they often lived in dirty, unhealthy conditions. Roads and paths were muddy in winter and dusty in summertime. Individual homes, from castles to cottages, could be damp or drafty and infested with mice, rats, flies, and fleas. Towns and villages were smoky and smelly. Human waste was flung out into the streets, where it **festered** alongside pig and horse manure, rotting vegetables, refuse from butchers'

to Catch fleas, france, c. 1400

Spread two thick slices of bread with a paste made of quicklime [crushed, baked limestone mixed with water].

Stand a lighted candle in the center, and place in your chamber at night. Fleas will be attracted by the light, hop onto the lime, be trapped there, and die.

Excerpt by author from a late medieval French housekeeping manual [2]

shops, and many other kinds of garbage. This filthy environment provided an ideal breeding ground for disease-carrying **bacteria**.

Few towns or villages—and even fewer ordinary homes—had clean, piped water supplies. Instead, medieval women carried water from rivers, ponds, or streams, using pottery jars or buckets of wood or leather. They heated the water in **cauldrons** over open fires to wash dishes, clothes, hands, faces, and bodies. In summertime, boys and young men might go swimming to get clean.

Soap was a luxury; only nobles and royalty could afford it. Ordinary people relied on plain water, lye (a mixture of wood ash and soda), or sap from wild plants. They cleaned their teeth with salt or wood ash or by chewing twigs. They used a bucket as an indoor toilet or found a discreet place outside in a dark town alley or behind a country hedge. For toilet paper, they used dried leaves and grass.

Rich families had servants to carry water for them and regularly took baths in wooden tubs

▶ French peasants sit in front of a smoky wood fire to dry their wet shoes and socks and the hems of their heavy woolen garments. This scene, showing harsh living conditions in the European countryside in winter, was painted in 1416.

(lined with cloth, to avoid splinters) in front of large open fires or washed in pottery bowls of warm water. In castles and grand houses, they had garderobes (little rooms with seats over open drains that carried waste into ditches or moats) or closestools (covered buckets with seats) in their bedrooms. Both had supplies of hay or neatly torn-up rags nearby. Rich men and women smoothed their hair with fine-toothed combs carved from ivory. Poor people used coarser combs made of bone or wood. Rich people also chewed sweet spices, such as cloves, to freshen their breath and rubbed perfumed oils into their skin and hair.

Rich or poor, most medieval people owned few clothes. Shifts, or thin linen shirts worn next to the skin, were washed regularly, though they were difficult to dry in wintertime. Thick woolen garments, lined with fur for rich families, could not be washed at all. They were hung outside to air on breezy, sunny days or dry-cleaned by rubbing with absorbent **wheat bran**.

Homeless people, wandering beggars, poor travelers, and other outcasts had nowhere to wash and usually only one set of clothes. As a result, many were troubled by lice and fleas. Rich people also frequently complained that these people smelled.

Death All Around

Growing population, food shortages, illness, bad diet, and dirty living conditions all meant that many medieval people did not enjoy long lives. Infectious diseases and accidents, such as drowning, falling, or getting burned by open fires, killed almost half of all children before they were five years old. Children who were tough—and lucky—enough to survive to age twenty might hope to live for another twenty-five years.

Even among healthy adults, sudden death was all around. Young men died from war wounds, accidents, or work injuries. They fell from horses, were crushed under carts, cut themselves on farm tools, slipped on building sites, or were gored by wild animals when hunting. Many nobles were

SUDDEN DEATH, ENGLAND, 1453

"On Tuesday Sir John Heveningham went to his church . . . came home again merrier than usual, and said to his wife that he would go say a short prayer in the garden, and then he would dine, and straightway he felt a fainting in his legs and sighed down. This was at nine o'clock, and he was dead before noon."
Letter from Agnes Paston, a fifteenth-century English woman [3]

Medieval Vital Statistics

Children dying before age 15	50 percent
Main causes of death	infections, accidents
Life expectancy at age 20	25 more years
Average age of death (adults)	between 40 and 50 *
Number of people birth–age 15	50 percent of population
Number of people ages 15–50	25 percent
Number of people ages 50–75	21.5 percent
Number of people over age 75	3.5 percent

* Many men and women died in their twenties and thirties, women from childbirth and men in war and accidents. Others lived on until their sixties.

fatally injured at tournaments (mock battles fought for sport). Among women, pregnancy and childbirth were the most common causes of death. Old people suffered from painful **gout**, arthritis, and rheumatism and died from chronic (long-lasting) infections, cancer, strokes, and heart disease.

▲ Medieval artists created dramatic images, such as this walking skeleton painted in Flanders (now Belgium) around 1450, to express medieval people's awareness that death was all around. Most medieval adults—and many children—witnessed the death of a family member, neighbor, or close friend.

plagues and epidemics

isease and death were well known to all medieval people—so was suffering. Encouraged by the Church, most men and women tried to endure whatever pain and bereavement troubled their lives. Nothing, however, that medieval people had experienced before 1300 could prepare them for the terrible events that followed. First there was famine; plague arrived soon after.

Hunger and Cold

Between 1315 and 1320, there was a serious famine in Europe after several wet summers ruined crops growing in the fields. Historians think that the early 1300s were a time of climate change when temperatures fell, shortening growing seasons for crops and reducing the amount of high land suitable for grazing animals or growing food. In Europe, the weather got colder. At the same time, cattle suffered from murrain (a deadly disease), and there were outbreaks of dysentery (a stomach illness) and Saint Anthony's Fire (jerky movements followed by death, which was caused by eating a fungus that grew on moldy rye grains). Records of law courts reveal a sharp rise in crime during the famine years as people stole goods to sell for money to buy food. **Chroniclers** reported that in some districts,

parents even ate their children—though this may have been an exaggeration, designed to show how severe poor people's suffering was.

The Black Death

The famine was bad, but much, much worse was to come. From 1346 to 1353, a terrible **epidemic** swept across western Asia and the Middle East. The disease was carried by merchants traveling along busy trade routes to Constantinople (now Istanbul, Turkey) and ports in North Africa. From there, it spread throughout Europe. Only Iceland and the northern districts of Scandinavia escaped. People at the time called this terrible disease "the plague" or "the pestilence." Later, historians gave it a fearsome name—"The Black Death."

The Black Death was spread by rats that scavenged on cargo ships and in warehouses.

◀ Too weak to walk any farther in search of food, these starving men and women have collapsed and died beside a medieval road. This illustration is from a chronicle (list of important events) of English history written and illustrated in Flanders (now Belgium) in about 1470.

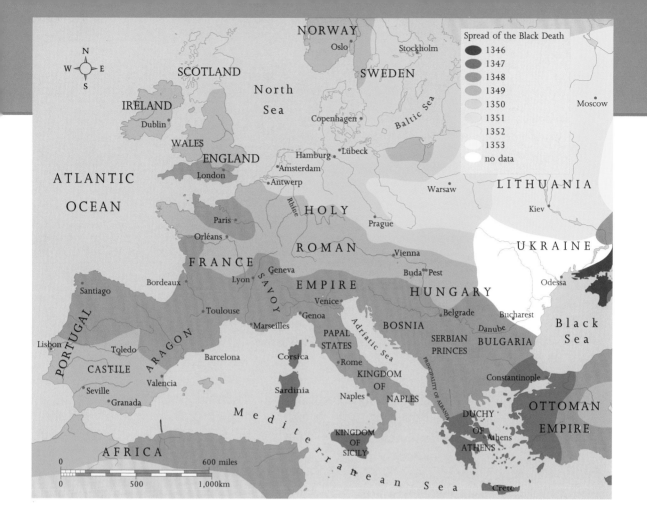

Spread of the Black Death

■	1346
■	1347
■	1348
■	1349
■	1350
■	1351
■	1352
■	1353
■	no data

▲ The Black Death reached Europe in 1347 from the eastern regions of the Black Sea and via the Ottoman Empire and the Duchy of Athens (today's Turkey and Greece) into the Mediterranean. From there, it spread north and south, carried by travelers, rats, and fleas. Within just a few years, the whole continent was infected.

They were infected with plague bacteria that lived in their blood. For most of the time, only a few rats had plague, but in some years, plague levels increased rapidly, and rats became a dangerous source of disease. The rats were also infested with fleas that survived by sucking the rats' blood. Each time a flea bit a rat, it sucked up some plague bacteria, which multiplied inside its gut. Rat fleas also bit humans, passing plague bacteria on to them.

The bacteria multiplied quickly in the human bloodstream, and the results were disastrous. Within just a few hours, sufferers developed high

◀ A bishop (right) blesses a group of monks (left) whose boil-covered skins show that they have been infected with plague. He hopes to comfort them in their last hours on Earth and help their souls reach heaven.

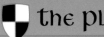

temperatures, dreadful headaches, and huge, painful boils called "buboes." In the later stages of the disease, sick people's bodies were covered with purple-black blotches, and they coughed up pus and blood. In a few cases, the infection passed directly from a person's blood to the lungs, then overpowered the whole body.

Plague was all the more terrifying since it struck very suddenly and because so few of its victims survived. Only about two out of every ten people who caught it recovered. Whole families—even whole streets and villages—were wiped out leaving dead bodies unburied. Historians estimate that more than half the population of Europe—between forty and fifty million people—died within seven years (1347–1353).

THE BLACK DEATH IN AN ITALIAN CITY

"Father abandoned child, wife husband, one brother another, for this illness seemed to strike through breath and sight. And so they died. And none could be found to bury the dead for money or friendship. Members of a household brought their dead to a ditch as best they could. And in Siena great pits were dug and piled deep with the multitude of dead. . . . And I, Angelo di Tura . . . buried my five children with my own hands. . . . And there were also those who were so sparsely [thinly] covered with earth that the dogs dragged them forth and devoured many bodies throughout the city."
Angelo di Tura of Siena [4]

There were also epidemics of other dangerous diseases. For the rest of the Middle Ages, however, plague was never far away. There were outbreaks throughout Europe, especially in big cities and trading ports. People who had caught plague but survived were immune to later attacks, so it was very often the children and young people born since the last plague outbreak who died. Many historians think this led the population of Europe to go on falling for many years after the Black Death and to start increasing again only after about 1450.

Medieval people did not understand what caused the Black Death. Most men and women believed it was God's punishment for their sins. Some even

◄ This wild, angry man was drawn by a fifteenth-century Italian artist to symbolize the planet Saturn. Medieval people believed that Saturn was evil and caused death and destruction on Earth. At the bottom of the picture, peaceful men and women gather on a city street. They seem unaware that Saturn looms threateningly over them.

thought it was a sign that the world would end soon, and there were reports that the Antichrist (the Devil) had been seen in eastern England. Medieval doctors said the plague had been caused by dangerous planets—Mars, Jupiter, and Saturn—passing through the **constellation** Aquarius on March 20, 1345. This had drawn "dangerous and corrupt vapors (gases)" from the Earth and spread them around the world, causing earthquakes and making volcanoes erupt as well. Less dramatically, medieval governments blamed citizens for leaving garbage and dead animals to rot in city streets, causing revolting smells and **miasma** (poisonous air).

In some parts of Europe, minority communities, especially Jewish people, were blamed for the Black Death. German preachers alleged that plague deaths were caused by poison dropped into springs and wells by Jews as part of a plot to kill all Christian people. Although these allegations were completely false, thousands of Jewish people were killed.

Medieval people had no effective treatments for the plague known now as bubonic plague. Even today, the plague can kill many of its victims. Priests led processions of barefoot, half-naked worshipers through the streets. They whipped themselves as they shuffled fearfully along to show sorrow for their sins. Doctors told people to burn sweet-smelling herbs and spices to drive away miasmas, to stay indoors when the south wind blew (they thought it carried infections), to avoid baths and sex, and to eat and drink very little. They said it was especially important to avoid "heating" foods, such as garlic and pepper, because they might encourage fever. "Cooling foods," such as cucumbers and spinach, were safer. They restored the balance of the body's **humors**, or life-giving fluids.

GOD MAKES MEN SUFFER

"Terrible is God towards the sons of men. . . . He often allows plagues, miserable famines, conflicts, wars and other forms of suffering to arise, and uses them to terrify and torment men and so drive out their sins. And thus, indeed, the kingdom of England, because of the growing pride and corruption of its subjects and their numberless sins . . . is to be oppressed by the pestilences."
Letter from a senior monk to the Bishop of London, September 1348 [5]

◀ A group of flagellants (men who whipped themselves to show sorrow for their sins) walk through the streets of a plague-stricken Netherlands city in 1349. Their leader carries a crucifix, showing Jesus Christ suffering and dying on a cross, the most powerful Christian symbol.

Plague Aftermath

The Black Death was probably the worst natural disaster ever to hit Europe. It caused horror, fear, massive loss of life, and countless individual tragedies. When the epidemic ended in 1353, the shocked and anxious survivors faced an uncertain future. Their families and communities had been shattered. Their loved ones were dead—so were their friends, neighbors, kings, queens, priests, local lords, and other employers. How could they rebuild their lives?

To begin with, most men and women went back to their old ways of working. It was all they knew how to do, and it seemed to offer the best chance of security. In the countryside, they paid rent to their local lord, or labored in his fields, or worked their own small farms. In towns, they re-opened inns, shops, and market stalls or took on fresh projects in their craft workshops. Plague survivors married each other for companionship and support and had children. Repeated outbreaks of plague, however, meant that old ways were no longer practical. By about 1370, there were many changes.

So few farm laborers had survived that they could demand—and get—higher wages. At the same time, rents for property and the price of food both fell because there were so few tenants or purchasers. Ordinary families could afford more food, warmer clothes, and better houses.

The Black Death also speeded up changes in medieval society that had started long before the plague broke out. Lords had increasing difficulty enforcing old claims made on **serf** families and faced peasant rebellions. Many workers left farming altogether and moved to rural industries, such as cloth or brick making. Others took jobs as servants, traders, or laborers in towns. Many parents and children no longer worked together on family farms.

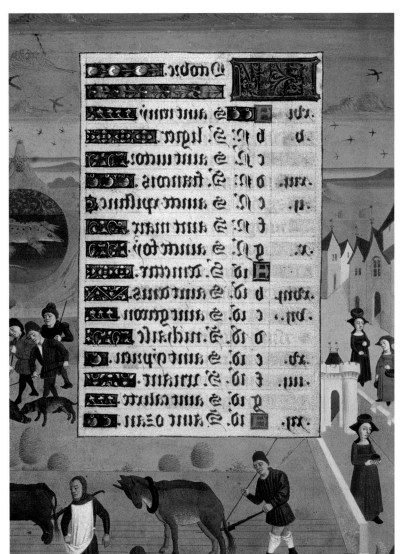

◀ This page from a French manuscript, painted around 1450, shows typical country activities during the month of October. Women shop and talk (*far left*) in a village street. Farmworkers plow fields (*front*), using a horse-drawn plow, and scatter seed in the freshly dug furrows. A group of huntsmen and their dogs (*far right*) have just caught a fierce wild boar.

▲ After about 1400, northern European towns, such as Lavenham in eastern England, grew prosperous through wool trading and cloth weaving. Merchants built fine new timber-framed houses (with oak beam and plaster walls and clay-tiled roofs) to live and work in and paid for magnificent new church buildings, where they worshiped on Sundays and at Christian festivals.

Rising Labor Costs and Wages after the Black Death

After the Black Death, labor costs increased sharply. Since there were so few people, workers could demand higher pay. Higher wages gave laborers more money but made farming less profitable.

	1348	c. 1380	% Increase
Cost to farm owner (in workers' wages and food) to cut 1 acre (.4 ha) of hay	5d*	7.5d	50%
General laborer's daily pay	3d	4d	25%

* d = *denarius* (the medieval Latin name for "penny," the most common medieval coin. It was made of real silver.)

Hay (dried grass) was one of the most valuable farm crops in medieval Europe. It was used to feed horses, sheep, and cattle in winter.

Lords and other rich landowners also faced big changes. They found that farming was less profitable, and their farmland was not worth so much. They invested in new **capitalist** enterprises instead, producing goods for wage earners to buy. Landowners' sons joined businesslike professions, becoming lawyers and bankers. Others went into politics or trained to become doctors.

In spite of the Black Death, repeated outbreaks of the plague, and many material changes, most people's outlook on life remained the same. They believed in God and feared punishment for their sins but hoped for eternal life in heaven. They mourned their loved ones who had died but believed that the living and the dead were still linked though prayer and might one day be reunited.

CHAPTER 3

Body and Soul

edieval people relied on many different theories to explain why the Black Death happened. Like all other medieval explanations of illness, these came from several separate traditions, mostly dating from before medieval times. The theories overlapped with—and contradicted—each other, but that did not worry medieval men and women. They were willing to consider anything if it explained their sufferings and offered the chance of a cure.

From Greece and Rome

One of the most influential theories originated in ancient Greece and Rome. It was based on the ideas of two doctors: Hippocrates (lived c. 460 to c. 370 B.C. in Greece) and Galen (who lived A.D. 129 to 199 in Rome). Both were pioneers. Unlike earlier Greek and Roman healers, who used prayers or magic, Hippocrates and Galen looked for natural causes of disease. They carefully observed their patients, making notes of the food they ate, the exercise they took, their characters, temperaments, environments, and lifestyles. They suggested that all these factors could bring health or cause disease.

Hippocrates and Galen also believed that everything in the world was created from four **elements**: fire, earth, air, and water. These elements controlled the seasons and the weather. They also controlled the four humors, which they also thought were found in human bodies: blood,

phlegm (mucus), choler (yellow bile), and melancholy (black bile).

Hippocrates and Galen thought that these four humors shaped each person's character. Even more important, they believed that the humors could sometimes cause disease. Normally, the humors were kept in balance within the body. When that balance was badly disturbed, however, by bad food, lack of exercise, poor environment, wild lifestyle, or unseasonal weather, then the body was unable to prevent illness.

After the Roman Empire collapsed between about A.D. 300 and 500, the Greek and Roman theory of four humors passed to new medical experts. These were Jewish and Muslim doctors in southern Spain, northern Africa, central Asia, and the Middle East. They made copies of ancient texts describing the ideas of Hippocrates and Galen and learned from Greek scientists, based in

Links with four humors

Medieval doctors thought that the Four Humors were linked to the elements, physical qualities such as heat, the seasons, and each person's character. They believed that understanding how all these interacted was the basis for good medical treatment.

Humor	Elements	Nature	Season	Character
Blood	Air	Hot and wet	Spring	Bold
Choler/Yellow bile	Fire	Hot and dry	Summer	Angry
Melancholy/black bile	Earth	Cold and dry	Autumn	Sad
Phlegm	Water	Cold and wet	Winter	Calm

▲ French doctor and scholar Guy de Chauliac (lived c. 1300–1368) is shown in this manuscript painting with three famous earlier doctors (*right*), whose ideas inspired and guided all leading medieval medical men. They are Galen (from ancient Rome), Hippocrates (from ancient Greece), and Abu Ali al-Husayn ibn Abdallah ibn Sina ("Avicenna," who worked in Muslim lands in about 1000).

Alexandria on the northern coast of Egypt, who pioneered the process of **dissecting** bodies to investigate disease. They combined these ancient ideas with their own more practical remedies.

Jewish and Muslim doctors also gained useful information from Roman army **surgeons** who were experts at treating battlefield injuries. They also learned from Roman engineers who understood that good sewers, public toilets, and clean water supplies helped prevent disease.

Greek and Roman medical ideas were "lost" to doctors in most of Europe for hundreds of years.

CURE FOR CONSTIPATION

"How can a young person heal his intestines if they are slightly constipated? If he is a young boy, he should eat salty foods, cooked and spiced with olive oil, fish brine [salt water], and salt, without bread, every morning; and he should drink the liquid of boiled spinach or cabbage in olive oil and fish brine and salt. If he is an old man, he should drink honey mixed with warm water in the morning."
Jewish doctor Rabbi Moses Maimonides (1135–1204) from *Rule of Health* [6]

▲ Holding a pottery jar containing herbs or spices, a Muslim **physician** (*right*) carefully prepares medicine to treat his patients. He is helped by an assistant who stirs the mixture in a large cauldron over an open fire. This manuscript was painted by a Muslim artist in about 1300.

They slowly became known again after about 1000, when Jewish, Christian, and Muslim scholars worked together in southern Italy and Spain. By about 1200, many scientific texts had been translated from Greek and Arabic into Latin, the language of Christian scholars. The most important was *The Canon of Medicine*, a collection of ancient medical knowledge put together by Muslim scholar Ibn Sina, known as "Avicenna" in Europe, who lived from 980 to 1037.

Stars and Sickness

The Greeks, Romans, and Muslims thought that sickness might sometimes be caused by stars and planets. Christian doctors working in eastern Mediterranean lands who had come into contact with Muslims combined the stars and planets with the theory of the four humors. They claimed that Saturn and Jupiter were evil planets that brought suffering and that Aquarius was a bloody constellation that could kill. Other constellations could also affect the body—from

the "Prince of Physicians"

Muslim doctor and scholar Abu Ali al-Husayn ibn Abdallah ibn Sina, known in Europe as "Avicenna," lived from 980 to 1037. Born in Bukhara (now Uzbekistan), he traveled widely, studying and learning. It was said that he began to treat his first patients when only sixteen years old. Ibn Sina also wrote about forty books on medical subjects. The greatest, *The Canon of Medicine*, published in about 1000, contained more than one million words. It gathered together ancient Greek, Roman, Muslim, and Jewish ideas about anatomy, health care, diseases, and treatments and became the most important source of medical information in medieval Europe. Ibn Sina was remembered long after his death as "the Prince of Physicians."

Aries at the head and Taurus at the shoulders to Pisces at the feet. The Moon caused mental illness, creating "lunatics" or dangerous mad people. Only the Sun brought health, strength, and life.

the four humors and the stars

Medieval doctors believed that each of the four humors was linked to the stars and planets. The four natural elements (materials from which the world was made) were linked to the humors and stars, too.

Humor	Star Signs	Planet	Natural Element
Blood	Aries Taurus Gemini	Jupiter	Air
Yellow Bile	Cancer Leo Virgo	Mars	Fire
Black Bile	Libra Scorpio Sagittarius	Saturn	Earth
Phlegm	Capricorn Aquarius Pisces	Moon*	Water

* Not a planet, but medieval people did not know this.

▲ This fifteenth-century drawing shows the four humors. The artist has portrayed them as four very different men with contrasting temperaments and physical characteristics: (*from top left, clockwise*) black bile, blood, phlegm, and yellow bile.

Natural Hazards

Most ordinary medieval people knew very little about the four humors or astronomy. Instead, they relied on practical knowledge and traditional superstitions to explain the causes of disease. They learned from experience that some plants and fungi were poisonous. They saw people perish from snakebites or scorpion stings or become weak from infection by intestinal worms. They believed that foul smells from toilets and garbage heaps caused sickness, too.

Traditional healers called "leeches" and "cunning women" studied all these natural hazards and tried to find cures for them. They also used natural substances to create potions meant to attract love, promote fertility, or poison enemies.

▶ Women gather lovage, an herb related to the vegetable celery, pictured on a page from an Italian herbal (book about healing plants) made in about 1390. Medieval people used lovage to treat inflamed eyes, upset stomachs, and many other complaints.

Elves and the Evil Eye

In the early Middle Ages, medieval people believed in another possible cause of illness—an attack by evil spirits or mysterious magical powers. In northern Europe, for example, the Anglo-Saxons believed that infections, such as chickenpox, were caused by "elf-shot," tiny arrows fired into the body by malicious spirits called elves.

In southern Europe, people believed that a glance from the "evil eye" could cause strong men to weaken and fall ill. The evil eye was a gaze or stare that superstitious people thought would cause harm. They also thought that if people meddled with witchcraft or magic, they might be possessed by devils. Then they would act wickedly or go mad.

Medieval men and women also believed that curses from powerful people could cause illness or even death. Breaking **taboos**, such as killing wild creatures, especially hares and spiders, or destroying trees thought to be magical like the hawthorn might also cause illness. Pregnant

MEDIEVAL "CHARM" (MAGICAL ADVICE) FOR GOOD HEALTH

*"If you wish to live and thrive,
Let the spider run alive."*

This meant, "If you want to stay healthy, don't kill spiders." It also carried a warning, "If you do kill a spider, something unhealthy will happen to you." Like many medieval superstitions, this charm had some basis in fact. Spiders living in medieval homes killed flies that carried diseases, such as food poisoning.

"Wise Woman"

The grave of a **pagan** Anglo-Saxon woman buried around A.D. 500 contained:

- twelve pendants filled with fragments of cloth, sewn up in a bag that hung around the neck
- a hollow deer antler
- a very sharp knife
- jewelry
- an iron pin
- amber and glass beads

Archaeologists believe that she was a "cunning woman," (a woman with an unusual or secret or perhaps slightly supernatural skill) and that the pendants were either lucky charms or used for magic healing.

women had to be extra careful of contact with the natural, and supernatural, worlds. They feared that their unborn children might take the shape of an animal or that their newborn babies might be snatched away by fairies and replaced by sickly, spiteful changelings (children who had been exchanged for others).

Sent by God

As the Christian Church grew more powerful after about 1000, its leaders tried to ban old superstitions and control traditional healers. They did not succeed. Church leaders were, however, successful in spreading their own view of the cause of illness. They said that God had sent sickness as a punishment for people's sins. They claimed that men and women were born wicked and suffered from original sin. They inherited original sin from Adam and Eve, the first man and woman created by God, who sinned in the Garden of Eden. Since they disobeyed God, all their descendants were born with original sin. When a person was baptized, he or she was forgiven for this sin. Original sin made people's bodies weak and their flesh liable to sickness or "corruption" (rot or decay or infection). The Church leaders also taught that the physical health of the human body reflected the spiritual health of the soul it contained. If a person was lazy or proud or cruel, this would sicken their soul, and their body would become diseased.

Some medieval Christian teachers went further and claimed that pain and sickness should be welcomed as blessings especially sent to help Christians. Suffering was God's way of purifying the soul and freeing it from sin so that it could enjoy life after death in heaven. Suffering should be accepted and endured with patience, bravery, and resignation, or obedience to God's will.

▶ This powerful image of God the Father, with angels and kneeling worshipers, was painted in 1397 to stand in an Italian church. When medieval people saw pictures like this, many felt ashamed of their sins and afraid that God would punish them.

GOD'S PUNISHMENT, c. 590

King Childeric I (ruled 561–584) of the Franks in northern France and his two young sons caught dysentery, a stomach infection that can kill. The king recovered, but both boys remained gravely ill. When their mother, Queen Fredegund, realized they were dying, she said to the king, *"God . . . has endured our evil goings-on long enough. Time and again He has sent us warnings through high fevers and other indispositions [illnesses], but we have never mended our ways. Now we are going to lose our children."* [7]

faith and healing

By about 1300, most people in medieval Europe had converted to Christianity. Their commitment to their faith varied greatly—so did their understanding of the Christian Church's teachings. Most people did believe, however, that diseases were sent by God. They also believed that God could heal them.

The Power of Prayer

The Christian Church offered several different methods of spiritual healing. The simplest, and most usual, was prayer. Priests told Christians to pray every day. Prayers should ask God for forgiveness from sin and include a promise to lead a better life.

Medieval people also prayed to **saints**. Over the centuries, some saints became famous for healing powers. Actually, the Roman Catholic Church instructed people to pray to God through the saints but not to the saints themselves. Church leaders explained that saints could ask God for favors for people who prayed, but all power belonged to God alone. Medieval people, however, ignored this teaching and prayed to saints directly. For example, women in childbirth prayed to Saint Margaret, sufferers from headaches prayed to Saint Denys, people with sore throats prayed to Saint Bernardino, and anyone who had been poisoned prayed to Saint John.

Charms, Relics, and Pilgrimages

Medieval people believed that, like prayers, holy objects could have healing powers. They carried little pieces of parchment with holy words written on them or bread blessed at **Mass** as lucky charms. They paid vast sums to purchase holy **relics**,

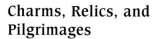
◀ Christian legends told how Saint Margaret was swallowed by a dragon, but miraculously she stayed alive. With God's help, she was set free from its swollen belly, as shown in this English manuscript painted in about 1370. Margaret's story made her a favorite saint with pregnant women. They hoped she would ask God to help their babies be born quickly and easily.

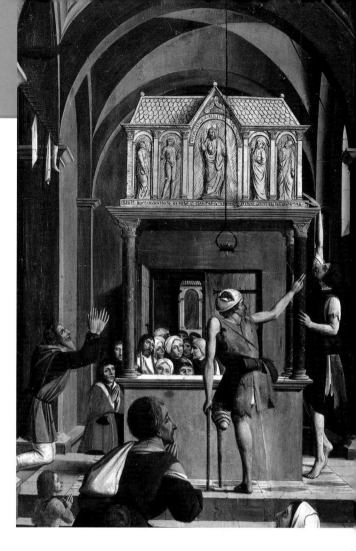

▶ Pilgrims with mental and physical disabilities pray for healing in a German church in 1498. They are kneeling in front of the tomb of Saint Sebastian, a saint believed to help cure plague and other illnesses.

such as belts said to have been worn by the Virgin Mary or a fragment of the cross on which Jesus was supposedly crucified. They went on **pilgrimages** to famous shrines, such as Walsingham in eastern England, where a noblewoman had claimed to see a vision of the Virgin Mary, or Compostela in northern Spain, where the bones of Saint James, one of Jesus' first apostles (companions chosen to spread Jesus' teachings) were said to be buried. They also lined up to be touched by French and English kings. The Christian Church taught that rulers were chosen by God and that this gave them healing powers.

Medieval Reports of Healing Cures

● About 1150, a boy named Robert, born with disabilities, survived by begging in Norwich, England. He moved from house to house on his knees. He was cured at the **shrine** of Saint William.

● About 1200, a young girl with mental illness lived a hard life on the streets in Lincoln, England. Local housewives gave her food. She was cured at the tomb of Saint Hugh.

Holy Charity

Priests also encouraged Christian people to give money, land, and treasures to the Church. Originally, these were meant to be a sign of religious devotion, but some medieval people came to see them as a way of making bargains with God. They felt that if they paid for a new church building or a gold cross or a fine statue

EYEWITNESS DESCRIPTION OF A MEDIEVAL HEALING RITUAL

"After the sun has set each pilgrim washes in Saint Thecla's holy well and tosses a gift of coins into it. Then he walks around the well three times and recites the Lord's Prayer three times. Next, he offers a chicken to Saint Thecla, says three lots of prayers, and carries the chicken three times around the outside of the church. After this, he lies on the church floor next to a copy of the Bible, drapes himself with a piece of holy cloth, and stays in the building all night long. In the morning, he gives Saint Thecla more coins and leaves the chicken in the church as an offering. If it dies soon after, people say that he will be cured."
Translated and adapted by the author from medieval English [8]

of a saint, then God would remember them. He might send them less suffering or cure their disease. Toward the end of the Middle Ages, the Roman Catholic Church employed officials to sell documents called "indulgences." These written promises were made for a fee by Church leaders on God's behalf to reduce people's punishments for any sins.

Doing good was another way for medieval people to win blessings and, they hoped, to be cured of spiritual or physical sickness. Church leaders taught that there were seven Works of Mercy that all good Christians should do. Medieval people also gave money to pay for places where sick or weak people could be looked after—leper houses or various kinds of hospitals. Some hospitals were run by monks or nuns;

the Seven Works of Mercy
1. Looking after the sick
2. Feeding the hungry
3. Giving drink to the thirsty
4. Giving clothes to the naked
5. Giving shelter to strangers
6. Visiting prisoners
7. Burying the dead

others were funded by charitable gifts and known as "God's Houses" or almshouses.

Leprosy (now called Hansen's disease) was a common disease in medieval Europe. It destroyed skin, flesh, and bones and caused terrible suffering. Since leprosy was incurable and seen as a punishment from God, lepers were treated with fear and loathing. They were not allowed to marry, had to carry a warning bell, and were driven out of cities and towns.

▼ Franciscan friars care for people with leprosy, pictured in an Italian manuscript painted in about 1380. Friars (brothers) were men dedicated to live a simple life serving God. Many followed the example set by Saint Francis of Assisi, who lived in Italy from 1181 to 1226.

▲ Monks and servants offer gentle care and spiritual counseling to patients at the hospital of Santa Maria della Scala, Siena, Italy, in 1441.

typical Rules for Lepers, c. 1250

- Do not enter churches.
- Do not go to markets, bake houses, or any place where people meet.
- Do not wash your hands or your belongings in streams or springs.
- Do not go out without special lepers' clothing.
- Do not sleep with any woman except your wife.
- Do not touch babies or young people.

The Church asked charitable people to pay for leper houses built at a safe distance from other homes. By 1250, there were almost twenty thousand across Europe. Most were run by monks and nuns. They provided lepers with food, clothes, and lodgings but no medical treatment.

Almshouses were lodgings for poor, weak, sick, elderly, or disabled people. Some offered shelter to traveling pilgrims as well. They were paid for by rich people and run by servants. Most had no medical staff, but they did have a priest who said prayers for visitors' souls.

Rich people could, and did, end up in leper houses, but most hospitals looked after only the poor. There were thousands of hospitals throughout Europe and more than twelve hundred in England alone. Many were run by the Christian

Church, stood close to **monasteries**, and were staffed by monks and nuns. Others, known as "God's Houses," often in big cities, were set up by rich people hoping to win forgiveness for their sins. The largest, such as Santa Maria Nuova in Florence, Italy, or the Hôtel Dieu, in Paris, France, had beds for more than two hundred people. The smallest had room for just five or six.

Some hospitals cared for people with special medical needs, such as pregnant women, babies, or people with mental illnesses. Most aimed, first and foremost, to look after the spiritual health of their inmates rather than to cure disease. Their patients were usually too old, weak, blind, deaf, or disabled to look after themselves or were simply poor, helpless, and homeless.

Priests encouraged hospital patients to think about God, while trained nursing staff— supervised by nuns—washed them, gave them clean clothes and bedding, kept them warm, fed them simple food, let them rest, and offered them medicines to ease their pain. The Hôtel Dieu in Paris had a staff of forty sisters, thirty novices, and sixteen servants. A pilgrim hospital, such as Saint John in Jerusalem, however, might be staffed entirely by men. A hospital for women after childbirth and a hospital for abandoned infants at the same site were both staffed by women.

DESCRIPTION OF A GOOD NURSE, FIFTEENTH CENTURY

Duties of the infirmary keeper at Syon Abbey, England, during the fifteenth century:
"She must fear God, work hard to show her love for Him, be skillful, strong, and mighty to lift patients up . . . know how to comfort them and encourage them, and urge them to confess their sins. . . . She must not be squeamish about washing or wiping them, she must not ignore their needs, or be angry or hasty, or impatient if one is sick, another has diarrhea, another is frenzied."
Translated and adapted by the author from medieval English [10]

HOSPITAL FOUNDED BY QUEEN ELIZABETH OF HUNGARY (1207–1231)

"In order to give shelter to pilgrims and the homeless, [Elizabeth] had a large house built at the foot of her lofty castle. In this house she cared for a great multitude of the sick, visiting them each day. . . . She shrank not from the sores of the sick . . . for the love of God. She applied their remedies, cleansed their wounds."
Jacobus (or James) de Voragine (1230–1298), Archbishop of Genoa [9]

In return for hospital, medical, and nursing care, patients had to listen to religious services (hospitals had chapels in most wards). Patients also had to pray every day for the souls of the hospital's founders.

A Good Death

Hospital care, however holy or kindly, could not cure most patients, so the Church taught that making a "good death" was also part of spiritual healing. When a person felt that death was approaching, they made or checked their will and called their family and friends to their bedside. They forgave all debts owing to them and tried to end any quarrels peacefully. They also summoned a priest. He heard them confess their sins, blessed their body with holy oil, and gave them holy bread to supply spiritual strength. Finally, the priest held a cross in front of their eyes while family members opened doors and windows to let their soul escape. Its destination might be purgatory (a place where souls were cleansed of their sins), heaven, or hell.

Many medieval doctors feared that this preparation for death would depress their patients and worsen their illnesses. They wanted them to have a more cheerful, positive outlook.

Nevertheless, after 1215 it was part of Church law that all patients must feel ready and willing to die before any major medical treatment. Most people made similar preparations before setting off on a long journey or going to war.

▲ A prince, a bishop, and leading nobles mourn beside the deathbed of Louis IX ("Saint Louis"), King of France. Louis died in Tunis, North Africa, in 1270, from a sudden infectious illness. Some medieval observers feared it might be plague. In this French manuscript, Louis looks calm and peaceful, ready to die in obedience to God's will.

medical professions

At the start of the Middle Ages, there were few trained doctors in Europe. By 1500, though, there were fellowships or colleges, professional organizations of doctors in most European countries, each with dozens of members. These organizations set high standards of education and training and tried to guarantee good medical practice.

University Training

Where had all these new doctors come from? Most had been trained at new universities. The first medical school was founded sometime between 1000 and 1100 at Salerno in southern Italy. According to legend, its first teachers were four wise men—a Latin scholar, a Greek, an Arab, and a Jew. This may not have been true, but it shows that medical knowledge from all those civilizations was known there.

Between 1100 and 1230, many more universities were set up. The most important were in Paris and Toulouse in France; Bologna, Padua, and Naples in Italy; and Oxford and Cambridge in England.

University training to be a doctor took at least seven years. Like all other university students, trainee doctors had to promise obedience to the pope and devotion to God. Like priests, monks, and nuns, they were not allowed to marry. They had to study religion, mathematics, astronomy, grammar (language), rhetoric (ways of presenting information), music, and philosophy as well as medical subjects. Women could not train.

The Church disapproved of too much dissection, but students practiced on animals, mostly pigs and monkeys, before watching their professors dissect humans, usually **cadavers** of executed criminals. Numbers of students varied, but, on average, a university might produce between one and ten fully trained doctors each year.

Physicians

These long years of study meant that qualified doctors were in great demand and could earn high fees. They worked only for the richest, most powerful people in Europe, such as kings, queens, nobles, and leading **clergy**. Most were physicians. They hoped to maintain their patients' good health and cure disease by offering them advice on lifestyle, combined with medicinal herbs and traditional treatments.

ENGLISH POET CHAUCER DESCRIBES A PHYSICIAN, c. 1390

"With us was a doctor of physic [medicine]
In all the world, there was no better
To talk of medicine and surgery
For he was trained in astronomy . . .
He knew the cause of every malady
If it was hot or cold or wet or dry
How it began, from which Humor . . .
Ready he was, with his apothecaries
*   [medicine makers]*
To prescribe drugs and all electuaries
*   [soothing, softening drinks] . . .*
At meals he was moderate as could be
Eating nothing of superfluity [excess]."
Chaucer's Canterbury Tales, Prologue,
the Physician **"**

▶ A medieval professor of medicine (*left*) lectures to a group of students. One of his valuable reference books lies open on a reading desk close beside him; three others are safely stored on a high shelf above his head. Two glass jars, for examining urine samples, stand beside his chair.

Physicians believed that men and women could cause their own sickness by living wickedly or recklessly. They could also improve their health by following a good and sensible lifestyle. To help, they offered spiritual counseling to their patients and discussed all kinds of problems that were troubling the patients.

For each patient, physicians drew up a rule of health, describing the amounts and types of food, drink, exercise, rest, and sexual activity they felt would be most suitable. This plan was not always followed.

Physicians also used their training in mathematics and astronomy to calculate healthy

advice not taken

King Edward IV of England (ruled 1461–1483) was a strong, handsome man, famous for his huge appetite and many mistresses. He allowed his physician to stand behind him at meals and encourage him to behave moderately. The physician was usually ignored, however.

and sickly times in each patient's life, when stars and planets would influence people positively or negatively from above. Too much astronomy,

▶ A fourteenth-century Italian **apothecary** offers a customer a jar of theriaca—a medicine believed to protect against poison. Jars full of healing herbs, oils, and ointments stand on shelves at the back of the store. The apothecary's assistant (*right*) crushes ingredients for more medicines, using a pestle and mortar.

though, could be dangerous; Spanish physician John of Toledo was accused of black magic and put in prison.

Physicians worked closely with apothecaries (druggists), who sold medicinal plants grown in Europe and costly spices, such as cloves and ginger imported from India and Southeast Asia. In 1236, physicians and druggists in Florence, Italy, joined together in a single organization to help one another. Many physicians invented their own medicines using traditional herbal knowledge, Galen's theory of four humors, astronomy, chemical sciences, and religion— or superstition—as a guide.

Surgeons and Barbers

A few university-trained doctors worked as surgeons—that is, doctors who operated with a knife. In southern Europe, they were often as respected, and as well paid, as physicians.

THE IDEAL SURGEON

"First, he should be learned, second, he should be expert, third, he must be ingenious, fourth, he should be adaptable. . . . He should know not only the principles of surgery, but also those of medicine [that is, being a physician] in theory and practice."
French surgeon Guy de Chauliac (1298–1368) [12]

In northern Europe, on the other hand, most surgeons' work was less prestigious and not as well paid. There were two reasons for this. First, southern European rulers demanded that all doctors should have some surgical training. This background was not required in northern lands, so well-educated, university-trained surgeons were rare. Second, there were already organized groups of trained **barber surgeons** in most northern European cities and towns. In London, England, there was a Fellowship of Surgeons by 1369 and a Company of Barbers by 1376. These practitioners had not been to a university. Instead,

they trained like other craft workers by being apprenticed to an older, experienced master. They went to work for him when they were around ten years old and learned by helping at operations.

Unlike physicians, barber surgeons practiced hands-on medicine. They stitched cuts, pulled teeth, dressed wounds and sores, applied ointments, lanced boils, stopped hemorrhages (sudden bleeding), gave enemas, and cut out tumors.

▲ A master surgeon (*seated*) reads from a textbook, while his apprentice begins to cut up a dead body. This woodcut was made in 1493 and entitled *The Anatomy Lesson.*

◀ A surgeon (*left*) uses a red-hot metal blade to **cauterize** a deep leg wound. The patient's agonized expression and near-fainting posture show that cauterization was a very painful procedure. In the background of this picture, painted around 1380, the surgeon's students watch and learn.

When a patient's life was in danger from infection or injury, surgeons also **amputated** limbs. Surgeons who traveled with armies became expert at treating battlefield wounds, such as deep sword cuts or embedded arrowheads.

Most barber surgeons were men, but women could train, as well. For example, in the fifteenth century, Katherine the Surgeon was recorded as working in London alongside her father and brother. Male surgeons often complained about women colleagues and about other women who offered traditional cures, such as herbs or lucky charms. In this, they were supported by many leaders of the Christian Church, who believed that women were inferior by nature.

Caregivers and Healers

In spite of these hostile attitudes, most health care was carried out by women. Poor families could not pay for expensive physicians, or even for cheaper barber surgeons, so mothers and grandmothers cooked and cleaned to keep their families as healthy as possible. They collected

AN ENGLISHWOMAN CARES FOR HER HUSBAND, c. 1420

"A man of great age, over 60, was coming down from his chamber . . . slipped or else lost his footing and fell down to the ground and his head was under him, and was grievously broken and sore . . . all streaked with blood. . . . Then his wife was sent for . . . she kept [looked after] him years after, as long as he lived, and had very much labor with him, for in his last days he turned childish and lacked reason."

An anonymous priest, writing the history of a medieval woman's life [13]

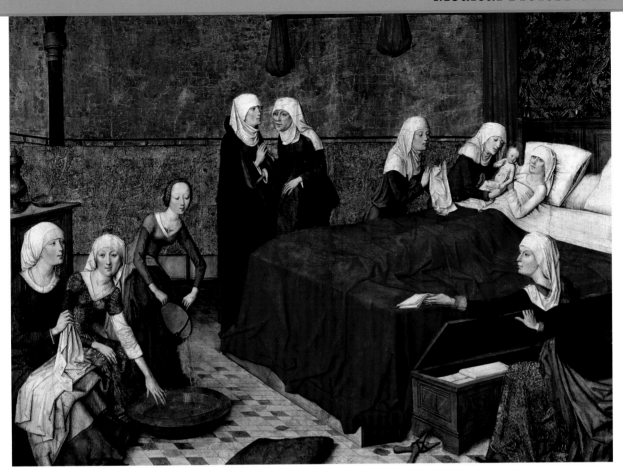

▲ A medieval midwife (*back, right*) lifts a newborn baby girl from her mother's arms, while a servant holds a clean, warm towel to swaddle (wrap) her. Nurses and servants (*left*) prepare a basin of warm water to bathe the baby. Another servant (*far right*) takes clean linen from a wooden chest. In this picture, painted in Germany in about 1470, two close friends of the mother (*back*) share a quiet word.

herbs and flowers to concoct medicines, mixed soothing drinks from wine and honey, made bandages from homespun linen, disinfected wounds with vinegar, and rubbed on ointments made of beeswax or lard. They sat up all night to comfort sick children or tend ailing husbands.

Female friends, neighbors, sisters, and mothers all comforted women during pregnancy and helped them give birth. Wealthy noblewomen paid female midwives to deliver their children. Being a midwife was a responsible position. It was physically tough and emotionally demanding—probably one in every forty women

A MIDWIFE

"*A midwife is a woman who has the skill to help a pregnant woman in labor, so that she shall bear and bring forth her child with the least suffering. And so that the child shall be born as easily and painlessly as possible she massages the mother's abdomen to help and comfort her. Also she receives the child as he is born from the womb and cuts the umbilical cord four inches long. She washes any blood from the child and massages him with salt and honey to dry and comfort his limbs, and wraps him in cloths and blankets.*"
Bartholomew the Englishman, c. 1250.
Author's translation from medieval English [14]

giving birth died. Medieval midwives did their best, but they were still mistrusted by medical men. By the fifteenth century, midwives in France and Germany had to be licensed before they were allowed to work.

CHAPTER 6

Diagnosis and treatment

efore deciding how to treat a patient, physicians, barber surgeons, and traditional healers had to **diagnose** what their illness was. Medieval health-care workers had no tools to see deep inside the body and no tests to identify disease-causing bacteria, viruses, or other microorganisms. Instead, they relied on examining the patient if he was male or listening to a verbal description of sufferings if she was female. They combined this information with reports from nurses and caregivers, careful observation of the patient's **symptoms**, and other vital signs, such as breathing, pulse, and heartbeat.

Testing the Waters

Most medieval physicians believed that testing "the waters" (urine) was the best way to diagnose disease. They used clear glass flasks, called "Jordans," to examine urine samples collected from patients at least once a day. They compared these with written charts prepared by medieval **scribes**, noting color, cloudiness, **sediment**, and other features. Many charts showed at least twenty different variations in the appearance of urine. Each one was said to show a different disease or to reveal a lack of balance between the four humors. For example, reddish urine suggested fever, while milky urine warned of dropsy (swelling caused by liver failure) and early death.

Physicians also checked each patient's pulse (ancient Greek and Muslim physicians identified more than thirty different pulse patterns), complexion, breathing, blood, and feces, eagerly searching for clues as to what might be happening inside the body. A physician or surgeon might even taste blood samples. Blood from a healthy person was said to be sweet; blood from a sick person was bitter or sour. Even stains left by blood on clean linen could provide useful clues.

All this information was combined with details of the patient's age, **rank**, character, state of mind, temperament, and lifestyle—plus the position of the Sun, Moon, stars, and planets; the season; the weather; church festivals; and the time of day. Only then did physicians feel able to prescribe a remedy, which might involve food, rest, exercise, massage, rigorous physical therapy, or medicines.

A Healthy Balance

Almost all medieval medical treatments were designed to cure by restoring the natural balance of the four humors in the body. In theory, an illness caused by "cold" humors, such as phlegm and melancholy, could be cured by warming "hot" herbs, such as camomile. Alternatively, too much heat caused by choler (yellow bile) might be treated by cooling herbs, such as lettuce, cold baths, or *infrigidative* (cold-making) medicines.

HOW TO IDENTIFY HUMORS

Gilbert the Englishman was a medical writer and compiler of one of the most widely used medical textbooks of the Middle Ages. He probably studied medicine in continental Europe. It is not known whether he actually was a practicing doctor.
"Put some of the blood on a linen cloth and wash away the blood, and the cloth will take on the color of the humor affecting the blood."
Gilbert the Englishman, c. 1250 [15]

In practice, though, treatment could often involve many separate medicines. The first batch "prepared" the body by strengthening it—many medieval medicines were dangerously poisonous. Extra "softening" or "ripening" medicines might

▲ This chart, painted in Prague (now in the Czech Republic) during the fifteenth century, shows flagons containing samples of patients' urine. Each contains a different color. The chart was made to help physicians diagnose suspected cases of plague.

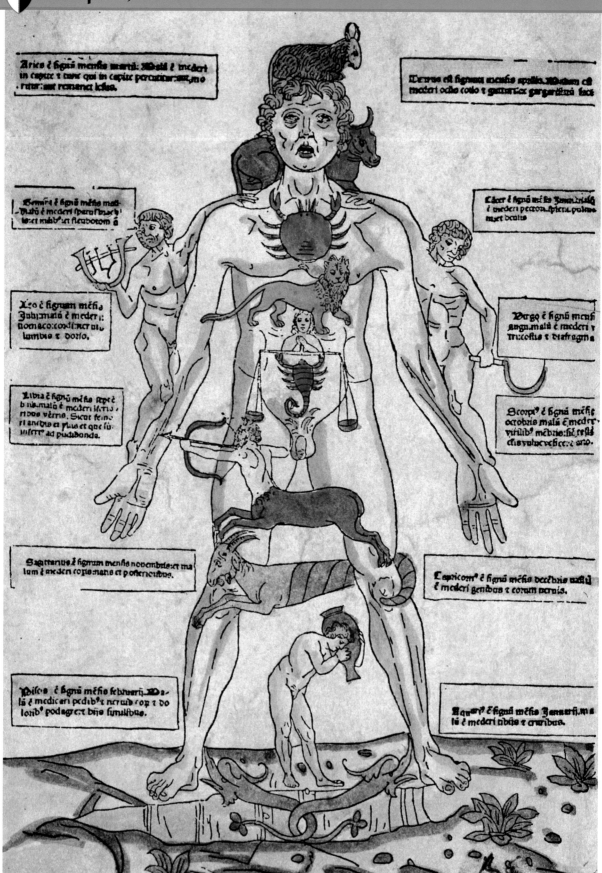

FEMALE AND MALE SYMPTOMS AND CURES

"If a woman's illness is caused by anger or unhappiness, try to make [her] cheerful, give her pleasant food and drink, and encourage her to take regular baths. And if it is caused by too much fasting or lack of sleep, make sure that she gets nourishing food and drink that will give her good blood, and encourage her to have fun and be happy, and stop thinking about gloomy things."

"If a man faints let someone bind his fingers with thongs and his toes as well, so that spirits and blood may be drawn away from the heart. And hold his nose, and open his mouth so that the fume [breath] can come out of his mouth. And wring him hard by the nose, and pull him by the hairs of his beard and also of his head. And let some friend of his kiss him who tenderly loves him. And rub his hand vigorously, and this shall make him rise up from his attack."
Gilbert the Englishman, c. 1250 [16]

Medieval medicines were made from a very wide range of substances. Some, like herbs, had been used for many centuries and had well-known powers. Mint aided digestion, for example, and rose oil soothed the skin. Other ingredients, such as crushed insects, must have been much less pleasant to use.

Medieval physicians—and traditional healers—believed that the natural world contained substances given by God that could cure all illnesses, if only they could be identified. With some plants, this was easy; they looked like the part of the body they were able to cure. For example, lungwort had leaves shaped and spotted like lungs and was used to treat chest complaints.

Food could also be an important part of treatment. Medieval physicians believed that fasting and purging could bring cleaning and healing. Good food encouraged the correct humor to be produced, but the wrong food could be harmful. Medieval doctors believed it disturbed "unbalanced" humors still further. Eating too much harmed the body in the same way.

be taken soon afterward to help break up any diseased matter inside the body. The next group of medicines **purged** the extra humor that was causing the disease and any softened diseased matter or rottenness that had collected in the body during early stages of the illness. The final group of medicines "restored" the body by rebalancing the humors and providing good nourishment.

Each symptom of an illness, such as headache or high temperature, might be treated with a separate set of medicines. As a result, a seriously ill patient was often given an alarming mixture of herbs, drugs, and other treatments. Patients suffering from the same illness might be treated differently because they had different constitutions (natural balances of humors) or different temperaments.

◀ This Zodiac Man diagram, made in northern Italy in 1493, was designed to show which organs of the body were influenced by different signs of the zodiac. When the Moon entered a particular sign, surgeons believed it was dangerous to remove blood from the corresponding part of the body.

fifteenth-Century Remedies

To cure a cough and cold, wash the feet each evening with hot water and then warm the soles of the feet in front of a fire and then take garlic and a little horehound [a plant] and mash them together, and rub the mixture on the warmed soles of the feet before going to bed.

To cure eye infection, take lots of pimpernel [a plant], crush it, and squeeze it in a cloth to extract the juice. Then take equal quantities of pig fat, goose fat, and chicken fat and melt them all together. Add the pimpernel juice and pour into a container. Rub onto the eyes before going to bed.
Excerpts translated and adapted by the author [17]

Taking Medicine

Many medicines were sipped from spoons, made into pills, or dissolved in wine or water and then drunk. Others were applied to the body as plasters (poultices covered with cloth), salves, or ointments. Some were administered as enemas, some were burned and inhaled, and a few were dissolved in hot baths where patients could breathe them as vapors or absorb them through the skin.

Under the Knife

Medieval doctors divided patients into two main groups—those with internal problems hidden inside the body and those with diseases or injuries that could easily be seen. Physicians usually dealt with the first group, surgeons and barbers with the second. Surgeons and barbers also offered first aid for accidental injuries and cut out, or cut off, diseased parts of the body when all other treatments had failed. In addition, they were responsible for the most widespread medieval treatment—phlebotomy (bloodletting). Almost all medieval people—rich or poor, educated or illiterate—believed this was good for them.

BLOODLETTING

"[Bloodletting] . . . clears the mind, strengthens the memory, cleanses the guts, dries up the brain, warms the [bone] marrow, sharpens the hearing, curbs tears, promotes digestion, produces a musical voice, dispels sleeplessness, drives away anxiety, feeds the blood, rids it of poisonous matter and gives long life. . . . It cures pains, fevers and various sicknesses, and makes the urine clear and clean."
A late medieval medical textbook [18]

To "let" blood, barbers and surgeons made a small cut in a patient's vein. The best place to cut depended on the illness being treated. To cure headaches, they cut between finger and thumb; to cleanse the liver, just below the elbow. They let at least a pint of blood, sometimes more, flow into a small bowl before applying pressure to stop the bleeding and bandaging the cut until it healed naturally. Like other medical treatments, bleeding was meant to improve the balance of humors within the body, but many people saw it as a general medicine to cleanse the body of "ill humor"—and from sin. They had blood let several times each year, especially in spring.

Bloodletting with knives was considered too dangerous for old, weak, and sick people. Barbers

◀ This illustration shows medieval surgical instruments from a French copy of a textbook on surgery, made in the fourteenth century. It was originally written by Spanish-born Muslim surgeon Abu'l-Qasim Khalaf ibn Abbas al-Zahrawi (936–1013), known in Europe as "Albucasis."

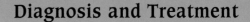

◀ A fourteenth-century physician cuts open a patient's vein and collects the blood that flows from the cut in a wooden bowl. Bloodletting weakened the body and could lead to dangerous infections, but most medieval people believed that it did them good.

or bowls. As the cloth burned, it used up all the oxygen inside the cups, creating a partial vacuum. This sucked blood from inside the body to the skin, creating red or bruised patches and often surface burns.

Other surgical treatments were even more painful. Cauterizing involved burning the skin with red-hot metal probes to seal wounds and stop bleeding, burn away diseased tissues, or drive away cold, wet humors that surgeons believed were causing disease. Surgical operations were the most painful and dangerous treatments of all. Most medieval surgeons would risk performing them only if they felt the patient might die if left without treatment. They usually asked the patient or his or her family to promise not to seek compensation if he or she died during the operation or if it went wrong. They also told the patient to make a will and to confess any sins to God.

and surgeons used **leeches** to suck smaller quantities of blood from the veins. Hungry leeches used their mouthparts to make a small hole in the skin, then sucked until they were full.

Blood was not let using knives from women or children, either. Instead, they were treated by a painful process called "cupping." First, their skin was scratched or scraped with a blade. Next, little pieces of cloth were placed on the scratched skin, set on fire, then covered with metal cups

A SURGEON'S DUTIES, c. 1500

"[His duties are] staunching blood, examining wounds with irons and other instruments, in cutting of the skull in due proportion to the outer skin of the brain with instruments of iron, couching [removing] cataracts, taking out bones, sewing flesh, lancing boils, cutting swellings, burning of cancers and similar, setting joints and binding them, letting blood, pulling teeth."
Thomas Ross, English surgeon, c. 1500 [19]

Medieval Anesthetic

- 3 spoonfuls of boar's gall
- 3 spoonfuls of hemlock juice
- 3 spoonfuls of wild catmint
- 3 spoonfuls of lettuce
- 3 spoonfuls of poppy
- 3 spoonfuls of henbane
- 3 spoonfuls of vinegar

Mix them all together and heat them. Add half a gallon (2 liters) wine and mix well together. Sit the patient in front of a warm fire, and make him drink until he falls asleep. Then you may cut him open.

This mixture was a powerful painkiller, but it probably killed many patients. It would also have tasted absolutely disgusting.

A late medieval recipe [20]

▶ This thirteenth-century manuscript shows a medieval surgeon cutting open a skull, using a hammer and a chisel. Operations like this, performed to try to cure mental illness or epilepsy, were just as likely to kill the patient as to cure him.

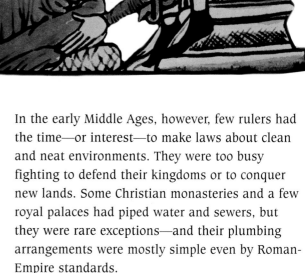

Patients undergoing surgery were tied up or held down firmly by the surgeon's strong assistants, who were especially trained not to respond to cries of pain. Before the operation, most patients were given herbal anesthetics (drugs that cause unconsciousness) to bring sleep and ease suffering. Most of these mixtures were very dangerous, however, and could easily cause death themselves. If patients survived the shock of the operation, their lives were still at risk from uncontrolled bleeding, blood clots, or bacterial infections.

Clean and Neat

Ever since Roman times, people recognized that clean surroundings and pure water supplies were good for health and might even help cure disease.

In the early Middle Ages, however, few rulers had the time—or interest—to make laws about clean and neat environments. They were too busy fighting to defend their kingdoms or to conquer new lands. Some Christian monasteries and a few royal palaces had piped water and sewers, but they were rare exceptions—and their plumbing arrangements were mostly simple even by Roman-Empire standards.

Toward the end of the Middle Ages, attitudes toward public health changed, and national and local governments made laws to clean up living conditions, especially in fast-growing cities and towns. The changes occurred for three main reasons. First, medieval European visitors to Muslim countries admired the sewers, public baths, and drinking fountains they saw there and compared them to their own dirty environments at home. Second, governments hoped that removing dirt and garbage would get rid of miasmas and prevent the return of terrible epidemics, especially plague. Third, towns and manufacturing became increasingly important to European economies in the years after the Black Death. Many people who moved to live and work there, however, quickly died. Town governments realized that they must make towns healthier places to live if they wanted to develop and become richer.

▼ Medieval travelers to Muslim lands admired the piped drinking water supplies and public baths they saw in Muslim towns. This Muslim manuscript, painted in 1494, shows men bathing, washing their hair, and changing into clean clothes, while an attendant hangs soft bath towels on a rack to dry. Muslim bathhouses also offered services, such as massages and haircuts, to help men stay clean, neat, and healthy.

SWEEPING STREETS, YORK, ENGLAND, 1332

"The king, detesting the abominable smell abounding in the said city [York] . . . from the dung and manure and other filth and dirt wherewith the streets and lanes are filled and obstructed . . . orders them to cause all the streets and lanes of the city to be cleansed of such filth and kept clean."
Letter from King Edward III of England (ruled 1327–1377) to the mayor of York, 1332 [21]

By the fourteenth century, many towns and cities throughout Europe made new laws to clean streets, build public toilets (London had thirteen by 1380), construct sewers and gutters, remove manure, and dispose of garbage, especially from butchers' shops. They appointed special officials to check on the quality of food for sale and to safeguard public health.

Great Failures?

These new public health measures could not end illness, although they did help reduce the spread of infection and make towns and cities nicer places to live. Like the rest of medieval medicine, they were based on careful observation of the world combined with great practical experience, limited scientific knowledge, and misleading ancient theories.

Medieval physicians, barbers, surgeons, nurses, midwives, and traditional healers were nearly all well-meaning people who worked hard to ease suffering and, where possible, cure disease. With hindsight, it can be seen that they were probably bound to fail more often than they succeeded. Still, their skill and dedication as well as the courage of their suffering patients can be admired today.

c. 500-800
Climate changes in Europe; weather becomes cooler.

c. 541-544
Epidemic (possibly plague) kills at least one million throughout old Roman Empire.

c. 800-1300
Climate changes in Europe; weather becomes warmer.

832
Muslim caliph (ruler) of Baghdad (now in Iraq) has ancient Greek and Roman texts copied.

c. 850
Paradise of Wisdom by Muslim scholar al-Tabari is one of the first Muslim medical texts.

c. 900
Anglo-Saxon "leech" (healer) Bald writes a book of remedies; it mixes prayer, magic, and superstition with herbal medicines.

925
Muslim doctor al-Rhazi dies. He wrote textbooks on medicine and spiritual healing and directed two great hospitals in what are today Iraq and Iran.

c. 1000
The Canon of Medicine is published by Ibn Sina (Avicenna).

c. 1000-1100
First medical school in Europe is founded at Salerno, Italy.

1013
Muslim scholar al-Zahrawi publishes textbook on new surgical techniques.

1067
One of Europe's first leper houses is founded in Spain.

1080s
New textbooks on medicine, combining Muslim knowledge with Christian beliefs, are written by scholars from Salerno, Italy.

c. 1100-1300
Many new universities are built.

1179
Christian Church orders that lepers should be cast out from society.

1204
Jewish physician Rabbi Moses Maimonides, who worked in Spain, dies. His book *Rule of Health* contained advice based on his practical experience.

1210
College of Surgeons is founded in Paris, France.

1215
Church says that Christians should make preparations for death before medical or surgical treatment.

1236
Physicians and druggists in Florence, Italy, set up combined guild.

c. 1260
Muslim doctor Ibn al-Nafiz discovers how blood circulates through the lungs.

c. 1300
Population of Europe is now about eighty million.

New hospitals founded by rich now care for more sick people than hospitals at monasteries.

c. 1300-1500
European cities begin to make rules for a cleaner environment.

c. 1300-1700
Climate changes in Europe; weather becomes colder.

1315-1320
Serious famine strikes Europe, leaving many weakened by hunger.

1347-1353

The Black Death (plague) spreads through Europe. Population of Europe falls to between forty and fifty million.

1368

French surgeon Guy de Chauliac dies. He wrote books on treating broken bones and torn muscles as well as an eyewitness description of the Black Death.

1369

Fellowship of Surgeons is founded in London, England.

1376

Company of Barbers is set up in London, England.

1377

Ports on Adriatic Sea set up quarantine stations. Travelers have to remain for seventy days after arrival to prove they do not have plague.

1414

French doctors describe influenza for the first time.

1452

First professional association of midwives is founded in Germany.

1473

Ibn Sina's (Avicenna's) *The Canon of Medicine* is printed.

1490

An anatomical theater opens at the University of Padua, Italy, where professors dissect corpses and discuss their findings.

Source References:

[1] C. Warren Hollister, *Medieval Europe: A Short History*, Wiley, 1964, p. 1.

[2] From E. Power (ed), *The Bourgeois of Paris*, Routledge, 1928.

[3] N. Davis, *Paston Letters and Papers of the Fifteenth Century*, Oxford, 1971, no 26.

[4] W. M. Bowsky, "The Impact of the Black Death upon Sienese Government and Society," *Speculum*, 39, 1964, 1–34.

[5] Quoted in I. Dawson and I. Coulson, *Medicine and Health Through Time*, John Murray, 1996, p. 64.

[6] Moses Maimonides. R. Porter, *The Greatest Benefit to Mankind*, HarperCollins, 1997, p. 101.

[7] Adapted from L. Thorpe (transl), *Gregory of Tours: The History of the Franks*, Penguin, 1974.

[8] Adapted from N. Orme, *Medieval Children*, Yale University Press, 2001, p. 90.

[9] Jacobus de Voragine. G. Ryan and H. Ripperger, *The Golden Legend of Jacobus de Voragine*, New York, 1969.

[10] Original text reprinted, in part, in C. Rawcliffe, "Sources for the History of Late Medieval England," TEAMS/Medieval Institute Publications, Western Michigan University, 1995, pp. 116–117.

[11] Geoffrey Chaucer, *The Canterbury Tales*, Prologue, The Physician.

[12] Guy de Chauliac. Adapted from R. Porter, *see above*, p. 118.

[13] An anonymous priest. Text is adapted from H. E. Allen and S. Meech (eds.), *The Book of Margery Kempe*, Early English Text Society 212, Oxford University Press, pp. 179–181.

[14] Bartholomew the Englishman, c. 1250. Author's translation from medieval English.

[15] Adapted from F. M. Getz, *Healing and Society in Medieval England*, University of Wisconsin Press, 1991, p. xxxv.

[16] Adapted from F. M. Getz, *see above*, p. xxxvii.

[17] Adapted from W. R. Dawson, *A Leechbook or Collection of Medical Recipes of the Fifteenth Century*, 1934, pp. 26, 156.

[18] Quoted in I. Dawson and I. Coulson, *see above*, p. 69.

[19] Language simplified from C. Rawcliffe, *see above*, p. 47.

[20] From I. Dawson and I. Coulson, *see above*, p. 70.

[21] From I. Dawson and I. Coulson, *see above*, p. 61.

amputated   Cut off limb to prevent infection

apothecary   A person who sells herbs, spices, and medicines

bacteria   Very small organisms (germs) that often cause disease

barbarian   An ancient Greek word used by Romans and later Europeans to describe foreigners. It suggests that foreigners are wild, brutal, and savage.

barber surgeons   Surgeons without university training

cadavers   Dead bodies used by medical students for dissection

capitalist   A type of economic organization based on making, investing, and owning money

caravans   Travelers who group together to help each other, usually in a hostile region, such as a desert

cauldron   A large iron cooking pot hung above a fire

cauterize   To press red-hot irons into flesh to stop bleeding or to burn out disease

chroniclers   Scribes (mostly monks) who wrote detailed accounts of events

clergy   The group of people who perform the rites and have duties within a church organization, such as priests, bishops, nuns, and monks

constellation   A pattern of stars in the sky as seen by observers on Earth

Crusades   Wars fought between Christians and Muslims, pagans, or heretics

diagnose   To recognize a disease and suggest remedies

dissecting   Cutting up dead bodies to study them

dysentery   A disease that causes serious vomiting and diarrhea

elements   Basic substances, such as earth, air, fire, and water

epidemic   A widespread outbreak of disease

festered   Rotted and decayed

gentry   People below noble class who may have worked as royal local officials or, perhaps, as lawyers. Some were knights.

gout   An illness that causes red, painful swelling in joints, especially in the feet

humors   Life-giving fluids, which ancient Greek, Roman, and medieval doctors believed brought health or caused illness in the human body

leeches   Flat worms with suckers that suck out blood

leprosy   A serious illness that destroys skin, flesh, and bones

life expectancy   The number of years a person might normally expect to live

malaria   A disease carried by mosquitoes that breed in shallow water. It causes high fever and death.

Mass   The religious rite that includes the ritual eating of bread and drinking of wine, which is part of Catholic services; the two substances symbolize the body and blood of Jesus. The ritual recalls the last meal he shared with his apostles.

medieval   A word that relates or refers to the Middle Ages

miasma   Vapor thought to cause disease

monasteries   Religious communities where either monks or nuns lived, shut away from the rest of the world, to devote their lives to God

pagan   A follower of a religion with many gods or someone who has little or no religion

parliaments   Conferences to discuss public affairs, or the organization of political groups to form a government

physician   A doctor who treated patients with medicines, physical therapy, and lifestyle advice

pilgrimages   Religious journeys to a holy place

plague   A deadly disease caused by bacteria that live in the blood of rats and other animals; passed on by rat fleas

purged   Discharged from the body as waste

rank   A position in society

relics   The physical remains of holy men and women

Roman Empire   The people and lands that belonged to ancient Rome, consisting of most of southern Europe and northern Africa from Britain to the Middle East

saints   People identified by the Church as especially holy; ordinary people pray to them, asking for help with particular problems or concerns.

scavenged   found and stole something useful or edible among the weeds, the refuse, or the garbage

scribes   Professionals who made a living by reading and writing

sediment   Small solid particles at the bottom of a liquid

seed corn   Grain stored carefully to plant to grow crops next season

serf   Either legally belonging to a medieval lord, almost like a slave, or legally bound to work for a medieval lord on his land

shrine   A holy place, often linked to a saint

surgeons   Doctors who operated on patients, let blood, and carried out other "hands-on" treatments

symptoms   Physical signs of disease

taboos   Traditional rules or customs forbidding certain actions for fear of damaging consequences

tuberculosis   A serious disease that attacks the lungs and other organs. In the Middle Ages, it was fatal.

wheat bran   The soft, papery outer skin of grains of wheat

Further Information

Books:

Dawson, Ian. *Medicine in the Middle Ages*. New York: Enchanted Books, 2005.
Emmeluth, Donald. *Plague*. Philadelphia: Chelsea House, 2005.
Peters, Stephanie True. *The Black Death*. New York: Benchmark Books, 2005.

Web Sites:

The Great Famine (1315–1317) and the Black Death (1346–1351)
www.ku.edu/kansas/medieval/108/lectures/black_death.html
This is a very clear lecture by an eminent historian, Lyon Harry Nelson, professor of medieval history at the University of Kansas, including a map of the Black Death's spread in Europe.

Health
www.learner.org/exhibits/middleages/health.html
An overview of medieval health that contains short essays on who was treated and why, humors, and surgery.

Medieval Medicine
www.intermaggie.com/med/index.php
This clearly written web site for adults includes links to ailments and cures and to social connections with medicine, for example, religion, miracles, women, and education.

Story of the Black Death
www.click2disasters.com/black_death/black_death_ch1.htm
This is a web site dedicated solely to the Black Death and all its aspects in short chapters. There is information on where the disease originated, how the structure of society broke down, the scapegoats, and what happened afterward.